West Federal Taxation An Introduction to Business Entities, 2002 Edition
by Smith, Raabe, Maloney

| | |
|---|---|
| Acquisitions Editor: | Scott Person |
| Developmental Editor: | Rebecca von Gillern |
| Marketing Manager: | Jennifer Codner |
| Production Editor: | Marcella Dechter |
| Manufacturing Coordinator: | Doug Wilke |
| Internal Design: | Carolyn Deacy Design, San Francisco |
| Cover Design: | Paul Neff Design, Cincinnati |
| Production House: | Litten Editing and Production—Peggy Shelton |
| Compositor: | Texterity, Inc. |
| Printer: | Von Hoffmann Press, Inc. |

Printed in the United States of America
1 2 3 4 5 04 03 02 01

For more information contact South-Western College Publishing, 5101 Madison Road, Cincinnati, Ohio, 45227 or find us on the Internet at http://www.swcollege.com

**For permission to use material from this text or product, contact us by**
• **telephone: 1-800-730-2214**
• **fax: 1-800-730-2215**
• **web: http://www.thomsonrights.com**

**Library of Congress Cataloging-in-Publication Data**

ISBN 0–324–11053–7

ISSN 1093–5134
2002 ANNUAL EDITION

This book is printed on acid-free paper.

## Basic Standard Deduction Amounts

| Filing Status | Standard Deduction Amount | |
|---|---|---|
| | 2000 | 2001 |
| Single | $4,400 | $4,550 |
| Married, filing jointly | 7,350 | 7,600 |
| Surviving spouse | 7,350 | 7,600 |
| Head of household | 6,450 | 6,650 |
| Married, filing separately | 3,675 | 3,800 |

## Amount of Each Additional Standard Deduction

| Filing Status | 2000 | 2001 |
|---|---|---|
| Single | $1,100 | $1,100 |
| Married, filing jointly | 850 | 900 |
| Surviving spouse | 850 | 900 |
| Head of household | 1,100 | 1,100 |
| Married, filing separately | 850 | 900 |

## Personal and Dependency Exemption

| 2000 | 2001 |
|---|---|
| $2,800 | $2,900 |

## Income Tax Rates—Corporations

| Taxable Income | Tax Rate |
|---|---|
| Not over $50,000 | 15% |
| Over $50,000 but not over $75,000 | 25% |
| Over $75,000 but not over $100,000 | 34% |
| Over $100,000 but not over $335,000 | 39%* |
| Over $335,000 but not over $10,000,000 | 34% |
| Over $10,000,000 but not over $15,000,000 | 35% |
| Over $15,000,000 but not over $18,333,333 | 38%** |
| Over $18,333,333 | 35% |

*Five percent of this rate represents a phase-out of the benefits of the lower tax rates on the first $75,000 of taxable income.
**Three percent of this rate represents a phase-out of the benefits of the lower tax rate (34% rather than 35%) on the first $10 million of taxable income.

# West Federal Taxatio[n]

# An Introductio[n to]
# Business Entiti[es]

# 2 0 0 2
## E D I T I O N

### General Editors

**James E. Smith**
Ph.D., C.P.A.
College of William and Mary

**William A. Raabe**
Ph.D., C.P.A.
Capital University

**Davi[d]**
Ph[.D.,]
Univer[sity]

### Authors for West Federal Taxation Series

**James H. Boyd**
Ph.D., C.P.A.
Arizona State University

**William H. Hoffman, Jr.**
J.D., Ph.D., C.P.A.
University of Houston

**Debra**
Ph.D
Washington [S]

**D. Larry Crumbley**
Ph.D., C.P.A.
Louisiana State University

**Mark B. Persellin**
Ph.D., C.P.A., C.F.P.
St. Mary's University

**W. Euge[ne]**
J.D., Ph.[D.]
Virginia Po[lytechnic]
Institute and St[ate]

**Jon S. Davis**
Ph.D., C.P.A.
University of Wisconsin-Madison

**Boyd C. Randall**
J.D., Ph.D.
Brigham Young University

**Eugene [W]**
Ph.D., C.
University of Illino[is]

**Steven C. Dilley**
J.D., Ph.D., C.P.A.
Michigan State University

## SOUTH-WESTERN
### THOMSON LEARNING

Australia · Canada · Mexico · Singapore · Spain · United Kingdom · United States